Brussels Beer City

*Stories from Brussels'
brewing past*

Eoghan Walsh

For more information, address: eoghan@beercity.
brussels.

First edition: September 2020

The following sections originally appeared in
Belgian Beer and Food Magazine: "A Tumultuous
Past", "Meneer Constant", "Brothers in Arms", "A
Battle for Brussels Soul"

Book design by Ruairí Talbot
Cover design by Ruairí Talbot

ISBN 9798666062746

www.beercity.brussels

CONTENTS

Foreword

Preface

A tumultuous past   2

Brothers in arms   8

Surviving Brusselization   20

Catch a falling star   28

A battle for Brussels' soul   36

The brewery at the European Parliament   48

Monsieur Constant   54

Build-A-Brand   68

Epilogue   82

Acknowledgements   88

About the Author   91

Notes   92

Opinion de M. Hetzel sur le Faro

« Buvez-vous du faro ? » — dis-je à monsieur Hetzel ;
Je vis un peu d'horreur sur sa mine barbue.
— « Non, jamais ! le faro (je dis cela sans fiel !)
C'est de la bière deux fois bue. »

Hetzel parlait ainsi, dans un Café flamand,
Par prudence sans doute, énigmatiquement ;
Je compris que c'était une manière fine
De me dire : « Faro, synonyme d'urine ! »

Charles Baudelaire

FOREWORD

by Joe Stange

We can time travel, you know. It doesn't work like in the movies, and it's not foolproof. But we can do it, with context and knowledge. A bit of period music helps, and some imagination. Sit in an atmospheric *fin de siècle* Brussels café, drink a glass of faro, and jump right into a book - not a book of myths, but a book of true stuff.

Belgian beer thrives on made-up stories and spooky folklore. It's not just cartoonish monks, gnomes, devils, phantoms, and witches. It's tall tales like the Kwak yard glass; the absurd founding year on a bottle of Stella Artois; or the "magic" of "spontaneous fermentation" from the Senne air (versus the very real science that unfolds in the barrels thanks to honed technique).

Myths are sexy, I guess. But you know what? Truth is sexier. History is sexier. I want to know what really happened. Because I want to time travel.

Sadly when it comes to Brussels brewing history - and especially when it comes to material in English - there are lots of blank voids and blurry areas. It's a dicey business. Personally, the era that intrigues me most is the city's heyday, the Belle Epoque, roughly from the 1870s up to the First World War. That's the era that formed the Brussels I love best—the gueuze, the Art Nouveau, the surrealists, the plucky Marolles.

It was also a heyday for brewing. One local enthusiast, Guy Moerenhout, spent a chunk of his life collecting everything he could related to Brussels brewing history. This included a fascinating list of every single Brussels brewery name that he could find from various sources, organised by municipality; he hoped that others would help him correct it over time. Sadly he died in 2014. I used this list to count brewery names active between 1890 and 1910, and found 250 different names. I have no doubt that most of those were tiny. I have no doubt that some of those were lambic blenders rather than brewers. I have no doubt that a few of those are plain old errors. It still strikes me as an exciting ballpark number. Even after the recent brewery "boom" in Brussels, we can still count them on two hands.

Here is another thing that excites me: Brussels was doing craft-style beer variety long before it was cool. In the year 1900 you could've drunk lambic, faro, gueuze, pale ale, brown beer, Scotch ale, stout, Munich lager, Bohemian lager, bock... Some breweries put out a diverse range, others specialised. Eoghan's work here helps me to see more clearly how that happened; it helps me to imagine what beers I might have found in which cafés, made by which breweries. It also puts faces and voices to names that linger like ghosts on buildings, murals, antiques, and in stories: Wielemans, Vandenheuvel, and so on. Thus history begins to un-blur, sharpen, and take physical form.

Myths are fun, I know. They're a pastime in Belgium. They also sell a lot more beer than history does.

But maybe, if there is justice, history can sell a few more books.

Joe Stange
Author, *Around Brussels in 80 Beers*
Co-author, *Good Beer Guide Belgium*
Managing editor, *Craft Beer & Brewing Magazine*

PREFACE

This book owes its existence to Paul Walsh (no relation), founding editor of the now-defunct Belgian Beer and Food Magazine. Not long after I published my article on Brasseries Atlas on my Brussels Beer City blog in September 2017, I received an unexpected email. "Would you mind if I republished the article?" Paul asked. Whether he was looking for last-minute content to fill that edition of the magazine, or had a genuine interest in Brussels' brewing history didn't really bother me. He was going to pay to publish an article I wrote, and it didn't really matter why.

That first article was followed soon after by a second, and somehow or other I convinced Paul to commission me to write a series of articles on the city's rich and varied brewing past, which would eventually be compiled into a collection and published for the magazine's subscribers.

That collection is what you're reading now. Sadly, the idea of this book outlasted the magazine, which Paul closed in the Spring of 2020. But before he did, he gave me the go-ahead to publish it myself. This backstory is not incidental; it informs the format and content of this book. Most importantly, that this is not a narrative history of Brussels brewing. That book is still to be written.

Instead, it is a weaving together of the stories and characters from Brussels' long-since disappeared breweries - charlatans, pioneers, and champions of their city - alongside contemporary observations on the traces these brewers and their empires left on the city. There is brewing, sure, but there is also architecture, social history, activism, football, urbanism, and more.

The history of the city's breweries is after all the history of the city, and while this is a disparate collection of brewery histories, even a cursory read will reveal common themes - the transformation of Brussels from a medieval backwater to a national capital, from a city dominated by artisanal guilds to an inner city engulfed by the industrial revolution, and the humiliation of the city (and its brewers) by a generation of rapacious developers and politicians that fundamentally re-imagined the urban space of Brussels post-1945.

As the title of the first story in this collection says, Brussels brewing has had a tumultuous past. But 2020 is probably (or was, pre-Covid-19) the most optimistic the city has been in half a century. For the first time since before World War I, the number of breweries in Brussels is growing again, and the city's residents have embraced the wide variety of beers that its brewers are making. As I write in the book's final story, and as this brewing renaissance takes hold, it is important to stop, take stock, and look back at the topsy-turvy history and see just how far we've come. And how lucky we are able to once again drink wonderful beers, locally made.

Santeï.

Eoghan Walsh
Brussels Beer City

A TUMULTUOUS PAST

Charting the history of brewing in Brussels through its vanished breweries

Number 10 on Brussels' Grand Place has a good claim to being the heart of brewing in Brussels. The building, after all, is called the *Maison des Brasseurs* and it is home to the Belgian brewers federation, a dinky little beer museum, and once housed a working brewery in its cellars. It's a ruse though; the brewers only moved in as late as 1951. To find the real heart and soul of brewing in the city you need to go in search of the River Senne.

There is still one place in the centre of Brussels where you can find the river. On Place St Gery, behind a forbidding metal gate is a small courtyard. At the base of the courtyard a lugubrious stream has cut out a small rectangle in between the surrounding buildings. This is the Senne, a pathetic sight now, but this stream is central to the story of brewing in Brussels. It was here that Brussels' medieval brewing tradition emerged, as breweries crowded around the river, siphoning its water to clean their breweries and using it to send beer to the outside world.

In the 19th century, when its occupants had soiled the river beyond repair, these breweries migrated to the rest of the city to build brewing dynasties that came to dominate Brussels. Throughout a tumultuous 20th century, they always returned to the source for inspiration. As brewing returns to Brussels after a too-long absence, it is worth looking back at this history to understand why brewing in Brussels looks the way it does in 2018.

A Guilded Age

Guilds and powerful brewing families dominated brewing in Brussels until the mid-19th century. In early modern Brussels, beer was sold out of the back of the brewery, and beers were named for the amount they cost or the colour – Braspenning, Roetbier, Waeghbaert. Napoleon disbanded the guilds in the early 1800s, but it took a surging population – which grew from 100,000 in 1830 to 180,000 in 1875 – for new breweries to emerge.[1]

By the 1870s centrifugal forces – overpopulation, pollution, and monumental public works that buried the Senne and reshaped completely inner city Brussels – were pushing breweries out of St Gery to the west of the city. More ambitious brewers looked further afield to the outer boroughs of Molenbeek, Anderlecht, Forest and Koekelberg where land was plentiful and transport connections much better.

By 1900 the city was entering a brewing golden age. The number of breweries had doubled, production began shifting from traditional lambic to bottom-fermented lager beers, and national brands began to emerge. Then came the one-two punch of successive world wars. The Great War erased half of Belgium's breweries, and Brussels did not escape the carnage. Breweries that survived post-Armistice Day emerged into an industry split into industrial giants – this was the era of Wielemans Ceuppens, Vandenheuvel, Leopold, and others – and a declining artisanal tradition.

Enter Schlitz, Watneys And Heineken

What the First World War started, the Second World War accelerated. Post-1945 consolidation was the order of the day, as big breweries swallowed up smaller ones; more than thirty breweries closed down between 1950 and 1960. Once the city's breweries had devoured themselves, outsiders moved in to buy up what was left – first Artois and Haacht, and later Heineken, Watneys, and Schlitz.

Even in these dark days brewers still returned to their ancestral neighbourhood, trading gossip and beer over rickety wooden tables in the cafes close to St Gery that now stood where the Senne once ran. But their time was nearing its end. When the lights went out at Wielemans Ceuppens – the largest brewery in Europe when it was built in the 1930s – in September 1988 the era of Brussels as a reference point for Belgian brewing was done. Only one brewery survived the killing fields of the 1970s and 1980s: Brasserie Cantillon.

Cantillon remained alone as a commercial brewery for nearly two decades, aside from a misadventure at a brewpub in Uccle in the early 2000s. It was not until Brasserie de la Senne opened their brewery in Molenbeek in 2010 that Cantillon had company. The River Senne was there again, in de la Senne's name and branding. In the intervening eight years a trickle became a veritable flood, as new breweries – L'Ermitage, En Stoemelings, Brussels Beer Project, and others – have opened, often sticking close to Brussels' traditional brewing neighbourhoods on either side of the canal.

Brussels in 2020 is alive with beer, and even St Gery is getting in on the act. The city's old stock market building, one street over from the St Gery market hall, will be transformed into the "Belgian Beer Temple" to tell the story of Belgian beer. A small brewing kit has even been installed in the St Gery market, brewing beer there for the first time in at least seventy years.

* * *

To understand how Brussels got here, you need to understand the rich history of 150 years of brewing, through the breweries that made it. And that is what this book sets out to do, telling the stories of the breweries that have defined Brussels – from the family businesses to the industrial giants, the local craftsmen and the foreign interlopers, the characters, the beers, and everything in between.

BROTHERS IN ARMS

The intertwined histories of two Brussels breweries

O n a late-October morning in 1997, bulldozers trundled their way through the sleepy Brussels district of Koekelberg. A wrecking crew was on their way to the corner of Rue François Delcoigne and Place van Hoegaerde to demolish Brasserie de Boeck, and with it all that remained of Koekelberg's brewing history.[2] Brasserie de Boeck's great local rival, the Grande Brasserie de Koekelberg, had suffered a similar fate a decade earlier. These breweries and their beers are now long forgotten, but together their stories embody an exceptional 150 years of brewing history in Brussels – from its medieval origins to its emergence as a 20th century industrial powerhouse, its transition from lambic production to pils, and the ruinous flirtation with modernity that was ultimately its downfall. Brasserie de Boeck and Grande Brasserie de Koekelberg saw it all happen.

They may have eventually suffered the same fate, but Brasserie de Boeck and Grande Brasserie de Koekelberg came from different brewing worlds. Brasserie de Boeck Frères was a family business, as most 19th century Brussels breweries were for the simple reason that sons of master brewers received a discount on their brewing studies. In the complicated business arrangements of the time, you could own a brewery but not brew there, not own a brewery but rent one, or – as Andre de Boeck did – own a brewery, rent it to someone else, and brew at your brother's brewery nearby.[3]

A family affair

This came to an end when Andre and his brother Pierre moved into adjoining breweries at the narrowing end of the Rue de Flandre in 1877. By the following year, they had merged to become Brasserie de Boeck Frères. They brewed lambic, faro, table beer, and bruin beer – "full-bodied and vinous, strong without being heady, pleasant to the eye and taste, particularly liked by 'those who do not like the acidity of faro'" according to Belgian folklorist Robert Desart.[4]

The brothers had ambitions for their new brewery, ambitions that involved them escaping the Brussels pentagon. It was just as well. Breweries all around them were preparing to flee the inner city. The River Senne that was once the lifeblood of these breweries had turned putrid and choleric. John Lothrop Motley, an American diplomat described it at this time as "the most nauseous little river in the world, which receives all the outpourings of all the drains and houses, and is then converted into beer for the inhabitants." [5]

The city administration determined to resolve this burying the river under new, *Haussmanian* boulevards in the 1860s. This not only cut off the breweries from one of their main transport routes, it also resulted in the wholesale destruction of over 1,000 buildings – houses, businesses, breweries – right in the heart of the city's brewing neighbourhood. The de Boeck brothers had by then bought up a plot of land in outlying Koekelberg, where they proceeded to build a maltings, warehouse, and a second brewery. By 1899 their brewery on Rue de Flandre was expropriated and demolished. Koekelberg would now be their home for the next seventy years.[6]

A German invasion

Koekelberg had always been home for the Grande Brasserie de Koekelberg (the clue is in the name). On January 15 1887, the first beers rolled off the production line at the "Brasserie de bieres Allemands de Koekelberg" on Avenue de la Liberté, on the edge of the Koekelberg plateau. These beers had strange, foreign names like Munich, Bock, and Petit Baviere; in fact, this was a Belgian brewery in location only. Everything else – the name (even though they dropped the "Allemands" within a year),[7] the brewery's director, the equipment, and the hops – came from Germany. This Teutonic emphasis was deliberate; their target market was not the traditional lambic drinkers, but the exploding local demand for bottom-fermented German beers. Before the 1850s Brussels had known little if any foreign beer imports. This changed abruptly in the latter half of the century as imported beer grew from 24,000 hectolitres in 1880 to 237,000 by 1910, [8]most of it German lager beers, Bohemian pilsner, and English pale ales.

George M. Johnson, founder and editor of the Belgian brewing bible *Le Petit Journal du Brasseur*, predicted that, before too long, lager beers "would probably ultimately oust the other kinds of beer completely, because there was comparatively no risk attached to their production in so far as their stability was concerned." Grande Brasserie de Koekelberg had one big advantage over their foreign rivals: freshness.

An 1888 newspaper advert promoted the brewery's beers as being "brewed exactly like the famous beers of Munich, with the finest hops. This beer has the advantage over imported beers as it has no need of any preparation for transport." It worked. The brewery sold over 32,000 hectolitres of beer in its first year.[9] The success of Grande Brasserie de Koekelberg wasn't limited to Brussels. At a competition in Munich in 1898, the brewery's gold medal-winning Munich Hähnebrau had Bavarian brewers running scared to the authorities complaining about the beer's authenticity and right to use the word "Munich".[10]

War Rations

Business remained good for both breweries, demand for German-style beer continued and De Boeck (and other lambic producers) had found in bottled gueuze – clear, stable and sparkling – a worthy local rival to this foreign beer.

Then came The Great War. The predations of war hit production hard with equipment commandeered for munitions, fleets of dray horses decommissioned, and Grande Brasserie de Koekelberg was forced to brew ersatz beer with beets, green beans, and peas. De Boeck and Grande Brasserie de Koekelberg spent the immediate post-war years investing in, and modernising, their equipment. Grande Brasserie de Koekelberg recovered to pre-war levels of production by 1920, and had comfortably surpassed them by 1926.

These interwar years were the last great golden age of Brussels brewing. The city's major brewing houses and their brands – Vandenheuvel and Ekla, Brasserie Leopold and Three Star, Wielemans Ceuppens and CTS Scotch – established themselves as national players and built themselves some of the largest and most advanced breweries in Europe. Competition intensified, as they sought to recoup the sizeable investments they had made. De Boeck tried to keep pace with these emerging behemoths even as lambic and faro fell precipitously out of fashion with local drinkers. In 1937 they merged with another brewery to form Brasseries Unies and consolidation of this sort would be the order of the day for the breweries that survived the next great upheaval – World War II.

Hubris and nemesis

Koekelberg's flagship breweries survived the World War II more or less intact, but never fully recovered. Post-1945 the challenges mounted for De Boeck. First the brewery had to deal with the consequences of a catastrophically hot summer in the late 1940s that decimated the city's lambic stock. Having survived this de Boeck then had to contend with consumer tastes shifting away from sour towards sweet, imperilling the popularity of traditional lambic and leading to the inexorable rise of the "capsule gueuze". Pasteurised, sweetened and artificially carbonated, the capsule gueuze was an innovation of Brasserie Belle-Vue – de Boeck's post-war bogeyman and a brewery that would come to dominate and almost completely destroy traditional lambic.

Into the 1950s and 1960s industry consolidation accelerated and breweries in Brussels fought like rats in a barrel. De Boeck and Grande Brasserie de

Koekelberg embarked on buying sprees in an effort to stay afloat and ahead of rival breweries. De Boeck hoovered up the city's remaining small-scale lambic producers and Grande Brasserie de Koekelberg merged with Grandes Brasseries d'Ixelles in 1954, becoming "Brasseries de Koekelberg et d'Ixelles", Ixelberg for short.[11] With Elberg Pils as Ixelberg's flagship beer and following the purchase of another brewery in 1962, production on the Avenue de la Liberté reached 250,000 hectolitres in 1965.[12] This was as good as it got. In the end, neither Grande Brasserie de Koekelberg nor de Boeck could spend their way out of trouble, nor stave off their better-resourced competitors forever.

In 1969 the house of cards collapsed. De Boeck finally succumbed to Brasserie Belle-Vue, who by then had cornered 90% of the lambic market. For Grande Brasserie de Koekelberg the end came in Christmas week. On December 29 Vandenheuvel – their great rivals who had managed to secure a seat on the Koekelberg board several years before – took full control and made the decision to close down the brewery.[13] It was to be a pyrrhic victory; a year later Vandenheuvel were bought out by English brewery Watneys and survived only five more years before being shut down themselves. But by then, Koekelberg's 90-year brewing legacy was already receding into folk memory.

* * *

Afterlife

The postscript for Grande Brasserie de Koekelberg is short. It left behind an unlovely functionalist building that was quickly taken over by a university for use as a cafeteria and study halls. In 1981 it was demolished completely to make room for a purpose-built brownstone, brutalist university building and by 2017 any remaining trace of the brewery was erased when that university building was in its turn razed.

Brasserie de Boeck's post-brewing life was a little more complicated. Unlike its neighbour, de Boeck was held up as a unique "exceptional" example of late-19th country brewery design in Brussels for its distribution of brewery and malting buildings around a cruciform central square. By the late 1980s it was one of the last remaining examples of 19th century industrial architecture left in Brussels. Brusselization – that word conjured up to describe the rapacious urban redevelopment of post-war Brussels – was the final humiliation visited on the city's now-defunct breweries. Few escaped its malign influence, and the ones that did were the exceptions – Wiels, Belle-Vue, and for a time, de Boeck.

It had been left to benign neglect since the early

1970s but that ended in the mid-1990s when Koekelberg's mayor Jacques Pivin identified it as his preferred site for a new housing development. Despite significant opposition from conservationists and politicians because of the site's relatively good condition and its historical importance, Mayor Pivin had his way. In the face of last-minute objections, it was under Pivin's orders that the wrecking crew were sent in that October morning, with a report claiming dry rot had made the place unsalvageable. As Guido Vanderhulst, a long-time advocate for the conservation of he city's industrial past, put it to *Le Soir* at the time: "What survived 120 years, was demolished on the pretext of a couple of weeks of dry rot."[14] The demolition crew were sent in one last time in 2003, to finish off a collection of buildings they had spared six years earlier.[15]

Today, Place van Hoegaerde is an anonymous, down at heel corner of Koekelberg towered over by social housing complexes. It's a quiet place; the buildings all around protecting it from the bustle of the main road and metro station two streets over. Of the de Boeck brewery only fragments remain. The cold neoclassical brewer's house that forms the sharp edge of one corner of the square is still there, abutted on one side by the old redbrick perimeter wall of the brewery. A black metal gate stands tall at the brewery's old service entrance; several years ago, barely perceptible from the rust, you could still make out the name of the brewery, but that fence has been re-placed.

For all his efforts to rid Koekelberg of its last piece of brewing heritage, Jacques Pivin never did get to see the pedestrian post-modern housing complex that rose up in its place. The honour of opening it fell to his son and heir, Philippe Pivin, who with no little chutzpah christened the new site "Les Brasseurs".

SURVIVING BRUSSELIZATION

The fate of Brasseries Atlas

B russels has not been kind to its architectural heritage. The process of "Brusselization" describes the "indiscriminate and care-
less introduction of modern high-rise buildings into
gentrified neighbourhoods" that characterised post-
war urban planning in Brussels and was responsible
for the callous destruction of historically important
buildings, whole neighbourhoods, and local communities. Brussels' breweries and their architectural
legacy were not immune. The Grandes Brasseries
Atlas is an exception.

"Le Petit Manchester belge"

As breweries shut down or moved their production
outside of the city from the 1960s on, most of
their buildings were torn down to make room for

an expanding Brussels. The few that survived this destruction were converted into art galleries, performance spaces, or hotels. Unlike its contemporaries, Grandes Brasseries Atlas in Anderlecht largely survived these waves of demolition and renovation unchanged. Cycle down the canal from the centre of Brussels and you can find the site of the old brewery in one of the old industrial centres of the city.

These are the neighbourhoods – in Anderlecht and Molenbeek – that comprised "le petit Manchester belge". Keep going past streets with names like Birmingham, Liverpool, Industry. Past the faded signs on crumbling brick buildings advertising "Ford" and "Coke". Past the old Moulart maltings complex that has been renovated as an interactive centre and a business incubator. And there, just along from the wrought iron rail bridge, is the art deco brewing tower of Grandes Brasseries Atlas.

The 30m-tall tower dominates this low-rise, working class neighbourhood. It is the central feature of the former brewery and is flanked by what were ateliers, multi-storey stables, a warehouse and offices, encircling a central courtyard. This courtyard was once covered, but the roof has long since been removed and on the day of my visit is populated by art-types working on various installations. All the buildings are more or less as they were where when Atlas finally shut down production at the site in the 1950s, minus the brewing equipment that was removed.

Brasseries Atlas - the story of Brussels brewing

The story of Brasseries Atlas is the story of brewing in Brussels in the 20th century. Brasserie Saint-Guidon was established in 1912 as a steam-powered brewery making Geuze and Lambic. In 1925, it merged with a nearby brewery to become Grandes Brasseries Atlas, at which point it shifted its focus to making pils and other lager beers.[16] The steam-powered set-up made way for the concrete brewing tower to house the new Pils-focused brewing equipment, but they continued to produce geuze.

Brasseries Atlas was caught up in the consolidation of brewing in Brussels after World War II; Brouwerij Haacht bought the brewery in 1949. The new owners shifted production of its Atlas brands outside Brussels in 1952 and converted the Atlas site as a warehouse and delivery hub for its products in Brussels. Any brewing-related activity ended when Haacht definitively moved out in in the late 1980s.[17] The site was then used as a storage and office space by a homeless charity. It is thanks to this benign neglect that Brasseries Atlas remains mostly intact today.

The tower stands tall above its surroundings, a tumbledown relic of a once mighty but now diminished industry. There is little extant brewing equipment left. Enormous circular cavities stretch up several floors that previously held 16 copper brewing vessels, now gone; missile silos long since abandoned. There is an eerie quiet to the building, as we ascend rickety iron staircases and avoid rotting wooden slats covering holes in the concrete floor. Scattered Jupiler cans suggest the tower still remains occupied.

A chapel for a koelschip
Two abandoned hot water tanks on the upper floors are more tangible signs of the building's past. The brewery continued to brew spontaneously fermented beers alongside its main production. Traditionally, the koelschip was placed on the uppermost floor of the brewery to allow air to flow through, cooling the wort and exposing it to the microbes that would ferment the beer. Here, however, the Atlas tower has an architectural quirk. Instead of placing the koelschip on the top floor, the designers built a small chapel-like room on one of the lower floors, complete with pitched ceiling and air vents.

The koelschip is long gone. Traces of it remain in shallow indents on the concrete floor. It is a still room. Close your eyes hard and you can get a sense of what it might have been like, wort evaporating into the night as chill air carried with it the germ of a new beer. One koelschip does still remain in the brewery, hulking and rust-red on the top floor of the warehouse building that abuts the tower. It is a relief to walk through the doors of the warehouse, escaping the midday sun into a cool, vaulted room.

We walk the cellars, crossing underneath the courtyard, and emerging in the atelier on the other side. It is completely dark save for my smartphone torch, which reveals the detritus of squatters and large pools of stagnant water.

* * *

What future for Brasseries Atlas?
The artists have moved from the courtyard to the atelier, where they have set up camp. They will not be there for long. Now that its final tenants have moved out, Brasseries Atlas' charmed life is coming to an end. Brusselization comes for everyone in the end. Housing pressures, a growing population, and the forces of gentrification have made it an attractive proposition for real estate developers.

Bizarrely, former Highlander star Christophe Lambert tried and failed to redevelop the site. Now it is in the hands of developers who plan to install a swimming pool and loft apartments in the brewing tower.[18] What are the odds that it will be just another isolated enclave divorced from its surroundings?

That neighbourhood is much changed since Brasseries Atlas' heyday. I leave to get a better look at the brewery's protected outer walls – Brasseries Atlas emblazoned in white against the red bricks. Meanwhile, congregants are filing into the recently built mosque next door to the brewery, answering the call to Friday prayers booming out of the crescent moon-topped minaret.

CATCH A
FALLING STAR

Expo 58 and the flameout of Brasserie Vandenheuvel

1 958 was a landmark year for Brussels, and an inflection point for the city's breweries.

For six months, all of Belgium descended on the city for the Brussels World Fair, and the city's brewers stepped up to supply them with as much beer as they could handle. Expo 58, as the fair was known, was the coming out ceremony of a modern, confident Belgium. And beer was central to this; the city's breweries had transformed an artisanal craft into an industrial behemoth ready to conquer Europe.

But, just as the Expo proved to be a false dawn for this now Belgium, so it was for Belgian breweries, a fall from grace exemplified by Brasserie Vandenheuvel of Molenbeek, the "star of the expo".

Expo 58 represented "the last moments of a prosperous, joyful, carefree, colonial and united Belgium." Opened in April 1958 on the Heizel plateau, the fair rode the wave of 1950s post-war optimism, showcasing new technologies and the wonders of the new consumer economy, across 200 hectares and 44 country pavilions.[19] Everywhere you looked, there was beer.

In the Expo's centrepiece, the Atomium, visitors could sit in a restaurant in one of the structure's chrome balls and have a glass of Vandenheuvel's Ekla Pils with their dinner. The "star of the Expo", Ekla was everywhere. It was Vandenheuvel's big shot at national success and a culmination of 100 years of brewing success.

From Saint Michel to Vandenheuvel

Vandenheuvel's origin is standard Brussels brewing history. The brewery started out in the centre of Brussels in the 1840s as Brasserie Saint Michel. Under director Henri Vandenheuvel, it grew quickly, being the first Brussels brewery produce dark, Bavarian-style beers.[20] That success led Vandenheuvel's successors to expand the brewery – now rechristened – at a 40-acre site across the canal in Molenbeek in 1920.[21]

Over the next 15 years, Vandenheuvel built a massive new brewery and introduced new beers: a stout, a bière de mars, and later pilsners, and Munich beers. By the mid-1950s, as Expo 58 hove into view, the Vandenheuvel brewery had tank space for 10 million litres of lagering beer fermented in vast open-topped tanks, and could package 45,000 bottles an hour.[22] In 1958, the brewery's output was focused on Heizel.

As part of the Expo, a folksy Belgian village was built, a comfortingly familiar sight for visitors arriving, and a way to send them home happy and well oiled with beer on the way out. In La Belgique Joyeuse – Happy Belgium – winding medieval lanes led onto baroque town squares flanked by renaissance town halls, behind which were streets lines with replicas of Belgium's art nouveau architecture. The streets and squares thronged with accordion players, magicians, singers, and organists.

Happy Belgium, happy brewers

In return for financing the village, a cartel of 32 Belgian breweries drew lots to receive one of 40 cafes where they could sell beer to the Expo's multitudinous crowds. Seven of these 40 served Ekla, from the Café William Tell, to the Cabaret Le Diable au Corps, and the Café Uylenspiegel. If you didn't fancy an

Ekla, you could trot across to the café of their local rivals Ixelberg for a half litre of Helles XL. [23]

For the more curious drinker, the national pavilions of other beer-making countries had plenty to offer. Pilsner Urquell on the terrace of the Praha Restaurant.[24] Whitbread's specially brewed Britannia Bitter at The Britannia Pub in the UK pavilion. [25] Waiting for you at the base of the Atomium were freshly poured ceramic mugs filled with Dortmunder Actien Brauerei beer.

By October 1958, 80% of Belgians had visited the Expo, and La Belgique Joyeuse welcomed 4.5 million revellers.[26] However, like the artifice of wood and plaster that was this Potemkin village, Expo 58 never delivered on its promise for Belgium or for Vandenheuvel.

The village was bulldozed, and the pavilions dismantled. Belgium ceased to be a colonial power in 1960 on Congolese independence. Already simmering language tensions between the country's constituent communities curdled in the 1960s, erupting periodically into unrest. Brussels was irrevocably transformed into a car-choked city.

A Falling Star

For Belgian brewing, the fate was even worse. Within a decade, many of the participating breweries disappeared unable to compete, or avoid industry consolidation. Vandenheuvel kept their head above water longer than most, absorbing some of its Brussels rivals in the late 1960s before being bought out by Watneys of England. Citing Ekla's poor sales, Watneys shut down Vandenheuvel in December 1974.[27] Save for an abortive attempt to revive the Ekla brand in the 2000s, Ekla and Vandenheuvel were finished.

* * *

Visiting Heizel now, the Atomium still dominates – even if you can't get a beer inside it anymore. Where La Belgique Joyeuse once stood is now the home of another ersatz tourist attraction – Mini Europe. Taking the curving tracks in the surrounding parkland, the rest of the plateau has been so denuded of Expo artifacts it's hard to imagine where the vaulting pavilions of glass and concrete once stood. In the place of The Britannia pub is now a clump of trees framed by rolling, grass hills.

Elsewhere, Expo ghosts do still linger. In an esplanade, scarred by age and neglect, that once soared between sections of the Expo but now ends in a chequerboard viewing platform. Or the American pavilion, a UFO crash-landed o the margins of the Expo site and recycled as a now-defunct theatre.

From the top of the Atomium, looking southwest you might make out in the distance the site of the

Vandenheuvel brewery in Molenbeek. It has fared even worse in the intervening years. The brewery was largely demolished once it was closed down. All that remained for a long time afterwards was a gaping hole in the ground where the brewhouse once stood, and an adjoining triangular building with the letters "VANDENH U ".

The building is slowly disintegrating, and a sky-bridge that once connected it with the brewery hung loose in the air at one end for years. Now, though, freshly sandblasted, this bridge connects to new apartment complex emerging from the brewhouse crater. The, development is capped by an 18-storey apartment block, dwarfing the buildings around but keeping Vandenheuvel's legacy alive.

Its promoters have named it Ekla.

A BATTLE FOR BRUSSELS' SOUL

The fate of Brasserie Wielemans-Ceuppens

I n October 1988 Guido Vanderhulst had storage problems. La Fonderie, the Brussels-based museum of industry and labour, which he founded two years prior, needed boxes for its archival material. Thinking beer crates were perfect for the job, Vanderhulst got on the phone to local breweries. When someone at Brasserie Wielemans-Ceuppens picked up, Vanderhulst received some very unpleasant news. "There are no more crates. There is no more Brasserie Wielemans," the person said. Wielemans' owner, Artois of Leuven, were shutting it down, stripping it out, and selling the land.

By the time Vanderhulst hung up the phone, he'd forgotten all about the crates. Instead, the frontlines of a fight were clarifying in his mind. A fight to save the last of the family-owned Pils breweries of Brussels. A fight to save an industrial icon from the city's golden age of brewing. A fight for a final sliver of the soul of old Brussels. In the months and years that followed, Vanderhulst was witness to political wrangling, the odd broken bone, and no little subterfuge. But on that October morning, all he knew was that he couldn't just let them destroy this brewery. "Wielemans is of the people of Brussels," he says. "We had to do something."

Crisp, clean and clear beers from Bavaria

The story of Brasserie Wielemans-Ceuppens is the story of how industrial brewing arrived in Brussels, and how it departed. Starting out in the city's old medieval centre as a brewer of lambic and faro, by the 1860s Wielemans followed its contemporaries in fleeing to the periphery in search of room for expansion. Under Constance Ida Ceuppens and her sons Andre, Prosper and Edouard, Wielemans settled on a plot of land in Brussels' Vorst district and set about plotting their brewing empire.[28] The change in location was matched with a change in direction. Their new brewery was built to produce the international styles that had become a riotous success in Brussels in the late 19th century – fresh, crisp, and clear beers from Bavaria and Bohemia.

In search of expertise, the Wielemans brothers barrelled through Germany and Austria, returning with a German-designed brewery and a head brewer from

Wurzburg to operate it. German-style beers soon followed; Wielemans was the first in Belgium to launch a blonde bottom-fermented beer, when its bavière and petite bavière were released in October 1885.[29] The beers were a hit, and the Wielemans brothers consolidated their growing dominance through expansion of production and constant modernisation and innovation at the Vorst brewery for the next two decades.

CTS Stout and Scotch

Their growth was halted by World War I. Occupying German soldiers stripped Wielemans of its copper, and restrictions on raw materials forced the brewers to use potato meal and beets in lieu of malt. And yet, two years after armistice and some canny investments from the Wielemans family, the brewery was back, pumping out 320,000 hectolitres of beer and about to lead the last great era of Brussels brewing.[30] As consumer tastes drifted from the defeated Germans to the victorious English, Wielemans adjusted accordingly. In the early 1920s they launched Crown Tree Stout, bottom fermented and named for the trees that lined the avenue in front of the brewery. CTS Scotch ale followed, and the success of these beers propelled the brewery to national attention and financed the construction of a new brewhouse.

What was built in 1931 was an art deco icon that came to define Wielemans in Brussels. A multi-storey brewing tower, it was the largest brewhouse in continental Europe when it was finished, housing two identical rows of four copper brewing vessels in parallel lines framed by double height glass curtain walls. It was, one contemporary commentator wrote, "a perfect modernism, from the industrial point of view, the most beautiful built in Belgium".[31] The brewing tower has stood there ever since, remaining largely unchanged in the intervening decades until it became the focus of Guido Vanderhulst's rescue effort in the 1980s.

Patrice Lumumba makes a cameo in Congo

With this statement of intent, Wielemans flourished. Leon Wielemans, scion of the family business and head of the brewery, became mayor of Vorst and lavished money on constituents and employees alike. Success was interrupted again by a second occupation of German troops in the 1940s, which reduced output and forced Wielemans, for lack of available manpower, to hire women in the brewery for the first time. By the 1960s the brewery had recovered once more, buying up several regional breweries, and expanding into soft drinks – once employing Patrice Lumumba, future prime minister of an independent Congo, as a sales rep for their Coca-Cola business in then-Belgian colonial Congo. [33]

Wielemans' green uniform-clad workers milled around on the streets outside, their work in the brewhouse blanketing the neighbourhood with the sweet, sticky smell of Wielemans beer. On most days, they brewed Wiel's Pils, the brewery's flagship that had started out as a so-called fluitjesbier – low alcohol beer, at 0.8° – during WWII, but re-emerged retooled and stronger in the late 1940s. It remained their marquee beer right through to the 1980s, its quality attested to by a neophyte drinker. "I was a huge drinker of Wiel's Pils, it was my favourite pils. Nothing super exceptional with them...the owners made a point of making a high quality beer," says Yvan De Baets, co-founder of Brasserie de la Senne. "And I can testament to the quality of Wiels for sure."

Enter the villains from Leuven

And yet, as the 1960s ticked over into the 1970s, all was not well at Wielemans. Belgium was buffeted by economic uncertainty and the city drew up plans to level the brewery and replace it with a parking lot or a metro terminus. Martin Vandenborre, the brewery's final technical director, told the in-house magazine of La Fonderie in an interview in 1990 that, even as they had hit a production record 538,000 hectolitres in 1976, "it was clear that the Wielemans brewery was condemned, in the short or longer term". [34] Vandenborre was unsurprised when, on summer holidays in Morocco in 1978, he received a letter informing him of the brewery's sale to their Leuven rivals Artois.

Artois kept Wielemans open while gradually shifting its activities to Leuven, and eventually shut down the brewery in 1988. In late September of that year, what remained of the workforce gathered to brew one last batch of Wiel's, a black flag flying from the brewhouse roof in mourning.[35] Artois was eager to move on, as they wanted the Wielemans site disposed of quickly. What machinery that could be removed was shipped to Artois headquarters, and the land was put up for sale to developers.

But Artois hadn't reckoned with Guido Vanderhulst. Speaking to him now, thirty years after that fateful phone call, it's clear that the passion drove him to prevent the brewery's destruction still burns bright. Vanderhulst returned to Brussels in the 1970s, after a childhood in Africa, to discover a city crumbling under the white heat of de-industrialisation.[36] It was a formative experience for him. He saw the factories that had dominated the Molenbeek district where he settled were disappearing, and the industrial heritage they were leaving behind was being left to rot. He saw the people that had worked and lived in the neighbourhood were fleeing with too.

The crusade to rescue Wielemans begins

"For me, it's man that interests me. The work. The machines, and the buildings, that came afterwards. I became an expert in industrial heritage because of working men and women," Vanderhulst says. From this experience grew his desire to rescue from oblivion the industrial fabric that had been brought to life by these people. It was a mission that led him to found La Fonderie, the Brussels museum of industry and labour. He set up the offices of the museum in a ramshackle abandoned ironworks, its outdoor areas strewn with a century of industrial flotsam, in a knot of Molenbeek streets behind the Belle-Vue brewery. It was from this redoubt, he launched his crusade to save Brasserie Wielemans from predatory developers and indifferent owners.

In the autumn of 1988, as Artois hired demolition contractors, Vanderhulst was busy. By the end of October, he'd launched a national media campaign against its destruction. He wrote that this was a battle not only for "a little of the soul of Brussels, but also its memory and its urban landscape."[37] When Artois saw the local media reaction, they accelerated their plans. They had already had to face down striking workers, resulting in the odd broken arm or leg of picket-breakers; Artois didn't want to drag out the process much longer.

The first things to go were the brewing vessels, to be cut out in pieces and sold for scrap. That's where Vanderhulst started. He got the ear of the contractor charged with their removal and convinced him to stall. Suddenly, the demolition crew began experiencing problems. "There was some complicity between him and me," says Vanderhulst. "I said, 'between you and me, you know, we have to save these.

So don't go too fast.' As a result, there were lots of problems, by accident or luck. They started cutting them [the vessels] from the top, they had problems. They cut a little bit, they had problems. Lots of false reasons. Because he understood we had to protect the cuves."

"Brasserie Wielemans was that important"

At the same time, Vanderhulst implored the mayor to step in and save a Vorst icon. He found another willing accomplice. "They understood the pressure that I put on them, the region, the commune," says Vanderhulst. "We placed the maximum pressure to make sure it was protected. The mayor did all he could to support me. Brasserie Wielemans was that important." Convincing Artois was a lost cause and, yo-yoing between Brussels and Leuven, Vanderhulst's objections fell on deaf ears. Artois did offer to donate the machines of the machine hall to La Fonderie, but were insistent that the brewery had to be demolished first.

Then, two months after Vanderhulst discovered the brewery was to be demolished, his campaign scored a critical success. On December 9, 1988, the regional Brussels government halted the destruction of the brewing vessels. Protected status followed in 1993 for the art deco brewhouse, the machine house, and the brewery offices. The battle to save the brewery was just the beginning, however, because now a question lingered: what to do with what was left standing? No one could answer with any degree of satisfaction; the site remained stuck in development purgatory for over a decade, as failed housing projects followed failed office plans.

Meanwhile, the land around the brewery flooded and descended into the swampland, and squatters occupied the art deco brewhouse. Eventually, the Brussels government expropriated the protected buildings. Following extensive renovations, in 2007 the brewhouse started its second life as the contemporary arts centre Wiels. The machine house next door became home to a cultural centre and Vorst's Dutch library a year later.

❊ ❊ ❊

"It was because of me"
By then, Vanderhulst had officially retired from the frontline fight. When I meet him in December 2018, he's sitting on a bench in the old machine house and surrounded by the unique 19th century pistons and compressors that have sat there for 100 years. Together with a cohort of volunteers and some European union funding, he's spent the past decade coaxing them back to their former glory.[38] He's surveying the room, evidently proud of what he achieved. "It was because of me".

And why shouldn't he be. For every Wielemans, dozens of breweries were demolished and with them a rich seam of Brussels folk history. Wielemans is special, it means something, not only for its architecture and its history, but because the brewery complex - or at least, some of it - survived when so many others didn't. Because of the fight in people like Guido Vanderhulst Wielemans didn't end up as one more tombstone to a forgotten industrial past. Instead it stands tall, incomplete but unbowed by time and its ravages. It is, once more, shining its light on the streets and buildings around just as its creators intended.

"We didn't completely win the battle," says Vanderhulst, a smile creeping out from under his moustache.

"But, what we did win wasn't bad."

THE BREWERY AT THE EUROPEAN PARLIAMENT

Brasserie Leopold and the "Whim of the Gods"

Rue Wiertz, in Brussels' European district, is a nothing street. Bound at both ends by slate-grey security barriers to protect the European Parliament, it is an unremarkable street in an unremarkable part of town. But, underneath the glass and stone towers that line the street, is a slice of remarkable history. This spot, at the confluence of Rue Wiertz, Rue Vautier, and Parc Leopold, is where brewing in Brussels died. More specifically, it is where Brasserie Leopold – the last commercial brewery operating on Brussels city soil – shut its doors in June 1981.[39]

Not that you could tell from the state of the place today. All that is left of the brewery – possibly – is a dilapidated redbrick wall on Rue Vautier that abuts an entrance to the parliament. It is a sad fate for a brewery that occupied this plot for over a century and one which shaped the neighbourhood around it.

Three Star Pils

Brasserie Leopold was originally Saint Hubert, brewing in the Elsene neighbourhood from the late-17th century onwards. In the mid-1800s the brewery owners were looking for a new site where they could grow the business. They eventually settled on Rue Vautier, opening the rechristened Brasserie Leopold (in honour of the Belgian king) in 1880. They soon shifted production away from traditional, spontaneously fermented beers towards increasingly popular beers in the German style. The first Brasserie Leopold bock beer was launched in 1888, and in the years that followed Brasserie Leopold built its business on the back of beers with names like White Star Pils and Three Star Pils.[40]

The Arrival of Artois

The brewery grew to occupy a plot stretching from the Museum of Natural Sciences to the entrance to the Bavarian State Permanent Representation on Rue Wiertz. It continued to flourish, but as the collective impact of economic crisis, increased competition, and industry consolidation accelerated, outside investment in the brewery was needed.

This external investment was the beginning of the end of Brasserie Leopold. In the early 1970s Heineken were brought on board, but they eventually sold their stake to Artois (of Stella) in 1976, which proceeded to do to Brasserie Leopold what they did to all of the Brussels breweries – they ran it into the ground. In June of 1981 Artois shuttered the brewery, laying off the 150 staff that still worked there and bringing to an end (for 30 years) commercial brewing in Brussels city.

"A neighbourhood that totally vanished"
It used to be that you could stand on Place du Luxembourg, next to the statue honouring British industrialist John Cockerill, look out over Gare du Luxembourg and see the smoke stacks and signs announcing Brasserie Leopold. Brewery and station were intimately connected; they shared a name, they shared rail infrastructure, and eventually they shared the same fate. From the 1970s onwards, the European Union's (then still the EEC) presence metastasised out from their base at the top of Rue de la Loi, gradually transforming a swathe of Brussels in the process. Jean Goovaerts of Brasserie de la Senne remembers "a neighbourhood that totally vanished around quartier Leopold" as the demolition crews dismantled the "amazing" brewing equipment.

In this context, a now-derelict Brasserie Leopold

and a run-down Gare Leopold were never going to escape the clutches of developers and politicians. The brewery complex did not share the good fortune of contemporaries like Wielemans in Vorst or Atlas in Anderlecht – breweries on unsavoury districts left to their own decrepitude. The real estate here was too precious.

"The Whim of the Gods"

By 1986 plans had been made to build the "Espace Leopold" as a prospective seat of the European Parliament in Brussels. By the mid-1990s the train station had been hidden underground. On the site of Brasserie Leopold was built the Spaak building, after the Belgian statesman, which houses the parliament's meeting chamber. This Spaak building was renamed the *Caprice des Dieux*, or "Whim of the Gods", by locals who saw a resemblance in its shape to the packaging of a local cheese brand. Only the old station hall on Place du Luxembourg remains, appended on both sides by glass walkways to the European Parliament.

❋ ❋ ❋

The vista from Place du Luxembourg is much changed now. The developers and the politicians and the bureaucrats have scrubbed clean any trace of the old life lived here. In its place is a dead zone of sanitized, wind-swept "public" spaces surrounded by soulless glass-and-concrete blocks, banal in their ugliness. Place du Luxembourg – or "Place Lux", or "Plux" – has become a playground for the youthful elite that works in these towers and in the surrounding streets.

The urban redevelopment that tore down the remnants of the old neighbourhood and transformed this part of Brussels is still going. Irish bars have been turned into salad bars, sports bars into organic beer bars. Café Marnix on Rue du Luxembourg, one of the few old-fashioned bars left, has been on the verge of closing down for months. It was finally shut and converted into a chocolate shop in 2018.

Back on Rue Wiertz, there are many memorials dotted about the street. To the ostriches that once lived here when the park hosted a zoo. To the creation of the Euro. There is even a piece of Berlin Wall plonked down between the entrances to Parc Leopold and the parliament. There is no plaque, no monument, to what was – until very recently – the last brewery standing in Brussels.

MONSIEUR CONSTANT

How one man defined Brussels beer, and football, for a century

C onstant Vanden Stock was a 20th century
Brussels titan. oted 93rd greatest Belgian of all
time in a public poll, the man defined football
and brewing in the city for 50 years. As patriarch
of the Belle-Vue brewery he transformed the Lambic industry, ushering in modernisation and pushing
traditional Lambic culture to the brink of oblivion.

As the president of Anderlecht football club, Vanden Stock was lionised as a folk hero, bringing the club glory at home and in Europe as he entertained Belgian royalty in the presidential suite of the stadium which carried his name.

The consequences of his market moves in football and beer from the 1940s through to the 1990s are still being felt today, and after he had retired from running Belle-Vue Vanden Stock sat down with Belgian journalist Hugo Camps to set down the events of his life. What came out of these conversations was a sort-of autobiography, the title of which sums up Vanden Stock's story: *One Life, Two Careers*.[41]

His life and those careers spanned seven decades, two world wars, personal tragedy, prodigious success and destructive hubris - and lots of trophies. In the rumble-tumble of Constant Vanden Stock, four dates stand out that defined his progress from café owners son to national icon - for good and for ill.

August 18, 1944

A bang at the door. German voices in the hallway. Philemon Vanden Stock is shook out of his bed at 2.30am. His name is on a list and neither he nor his son, Constant, know why. Three weeks later Philemon Vanden Stock is on the last train out of Belgium to the work camps in Germany. On September 3 1944, Brussels is liberated, but Constant can't celebrate: "Geuze has never tasted as hard, as bitter for me, as on that day." [42]

Philemon died in a German camp outside two days before the end of the war. Constant Vanden Stock never forgot what happened his father. "I would make sure that the name Philemon Vanden Stock would be known in the whole country, and if I could throughout Europe," he said to Camps in 1993. [43]

Constant Vanden Stock was always going to be a Lambic brewer. He was born in 1914, a year after Philemon started as a Lambic blender. In 1927 Philemon bought the Café Belle-Vue on Anderlecht's Place de la Vaillance and it was here that Constant Vanden Stock's apprenticeship began. He was serving beers by his holy communion, and aged 14 quit school to join the family business.

Constant's first major business decision came during wartime German occupation in the 1940s. German laws dictated breweries were licensed to brew a fluitjesbier, a 0.8% beer. Philemon refused to brew subpar beer, preferring instead to sell of what was left in Belle-Vue's cellar. Constant suggested an alternative. "If we add a dash of three-, four-year-old gueuze to the fluitjesbier, customers will be happy," he said.[44] Despite his father's vocal displeasure, business flourished.

In 1943, Philemon and his two brothers bought a nearby brewery and began brewing for themselves.

Anticipating his future diversions from Lambic orthodoxy, Constant altered their beer to make it more appealing as he saw it, harbouring greater ambitions for the growth of Belle-Vue than his father. "Even as a child, I remarked that some people found gueuze too hard," he said in 1993. So he "made it a bit softer and rounder" and broadened its appeal to new drinkers and securing the brewery's survival through the war. [45]

Christmas, 1969

Constant Vanden Stock has reason to smile. He has been running Belle-Vue for two decades. With the purchase of their Molenbeek rivals Brasseries Unies, Vanden Stock is now the biggest Lambic brewer in Brussels and set to expand Belle-Vue's dominance to Belgium and the rest of Europe. The brewery's success started not long after liberation in 1944.

Belle-Vue emerged from World War II healthier than its Brussels rivals, and Vanden Stock took advantage to break with the Lambic traditions of his father. His landmark contribution was the "capsule-gueuze".[46] Filtered, sweetened, and packaged in 25cl bottles, capsule-gueuze pandered to the sweetening palates of Belgian drinkers. It also saved the brewery from disaster. In 1949, a heat wave ripped through Brussels, destroying three million bottles of gueuze. Belle-Vue was spared thanks to its pasteurised, standardised bottles.[47]

The war behind him, Vanden Stock worked to "try everything to fill the emptiness that [his] father had left behind". As the brewery grew, Vanden Stock made sure the name remained the same: Société Belle-Vue Ph. Vanden Stock. Through the 1950s and 1960s Belle-Vue picked off their ailing rivals. "Left and right we bought what was for sale," said Vanden Stock.[48] Demand for traditional gueuze and Lambic was collapsing, and the city's remaining Lambic brewers had failed to modernise or win protection for traditional Lambic processes against innovations like Belle-Vue's capsule gueuze.[49]

In 1969 Vanden Stock saw a chance to tie-up the Brussels Lambic market. A merger between Brussels' Brasseries Unies and Brasserie Louis et Emile Decoster had left them debt-ridden and vulnerable to takeover. Vanden Stock made his move and, purchase complete, Belle-Vue moved into Unies' brewery in Molenbeek, which served as their headquarters for the next 20 years. Belle-Vue secure, Vanden Stock returned to his other childhood passion: football.

He had spent his childhood days playing in cobbled streets and nights curled up in bed with a football. Vanden Stock made his debut for Royal Sporting Club Anderlecht before his 19th birthday, in the Belgian second division. He stood out for his speed and his heading ability. "For anyone who looks closely enough at my forehead," Vanden Stock said, "they can still see the imprint of the laces where the ball was sown shut." [50]

He won promotion with Anderlecht in 1935, but a broken leg and the lost confidence of the team's management hastened his departure three years later. Vanden Stock swapped Anderlecht for the yellow and blue of their cross-town rivals Royale Union St. Gilloise, but the loss of his father cut short his career. "The first six years after the war I lived completely without football," Vanden Stock said. "Not one game, not one foot inside a locker room."[51]

Slowly, he inched his way back; first as trainer of the Anderlecht youths, then as manager of Forestoise, and eventually the national team manager. In 1969 his boyhood club drew him inexorably back to Brussels, and he returned to Anderlecht as a board member.

According to Jean-Pierre Van Roy, his erstwhile rival in Lambic brewing and then-owner of Brasserie Cantillon, there was the tantalising prospect that instead of Anderlecht he could have invested in his boyhood club across town. But, bankrolled by Belle-Vue's success, he became Anderlecht's president in 1971, launching an era of unrivalled success.

April 25, 1984
In the bowels of Anderlecht's Stade Ernest Versé, Brian Clough is quiet.[52] His team, Nottingham For-

est, has just been beaten 3-0 in a Uefa Cup semi-final by Constant Vanden Stock's Anderlecht. Clough is convinced that Anderlecht has bought off the referee. Before the game, his players claimed to have seen Anderlecht officials meeting referee Emilio Guruceta Muro's room. A dodgy penalty against them and a disallowed last-minute goal confirmed their worst suspicions. Forest player Garry Birtles said later: "It was embarrassing. Your natural thought is not that it was a bent referee, but we knew we'd been done."[53] Anderlecht's win against Forest put them through to their second consecutive European final and capped a decade of Vanden Stock-funded success.

Constant Vanden Stock was determined to succeed in football as he had in brewing. In their purple-and-white cotton jerseys, the circle Belle-Vue logo front and centre on their chests, Anderlecht won three league titles and four domestic cups in the decade after he became president of the club in 1971. As Belle-Vue stormed Europe, Anderlecht secured their first European trophy in 1976, beating West Ham Utd. to win the European Cup Winner's Cup and giving Vanden Stock "perhaps the most beautiful memory in my long footballing career". Anderlecht went on to next two finals of the same competition, winning once, before they defeated Benfica in the 1983 Uefa Cup to win Vanden Stock his third European trophy. Then came Nottingham Forest a year later.

It turns out that Brian Clough was on to something. Unbeknownst to either set of players, Vanden Stock had through an intermediary, paid the referee one million Belgian francs. He would later claim that they money was given after the game, and that it was merely a loan to the referee to help him with money problems. [54]

After the game, two men with evidence of the bribe blackmailed Vanden Stock for a decade. The payments stopped in 1996 when Roger Vanden Stock succeeded his father as Anderlecht president and discovered the blackmail scheme. He refused to pay and instead went public. Anderlecht was disgraced and banned from European football for a year, but by then Vanden Stock had secured his legacy as a club hero. [55]

July 4, 1991

On July 4, 1991, the almost unthinkable happens. Constant Vanden Stock relinquishes control of Belle-Vue, the brewery he spent half a century building in honour of his father Philemon, to Belgian brewery Interbrew (a merger of the Artois and Piedboeuf breweries). While his son Roger celebrates the take-over as "a marriage", [56] for his father Constant it's more like a wake. The elder Vanden Stock hasn't set foot in Belle-Vue since Artois bought a minority stake in the brewery two years previously. And once this decision is confirmed, he will never go back.

Belle-Vue's spending spree in the late 1960s and early 1970s meant that by the late-1970s the Vanden Stocks had cannibalised 80% of the Lambic market. And international expansion was next. "I still had one more debt to repay: to make the name of Philemon Vanden Stock heard abroad as well," said Vanden Stock.[57] France came first, with Artois as their distribution partner. Switzerland and The Netherlands followed, Belle-Vue failing only to break into Germany ("obstruction...pure protectionism") and America ("too careful"). [58]

By the end of the 1980s, the brewery employed 350 people, was producing roughly 311,000 hectolitres of beer a year.[59] Belle-Vue's size meant they had successfully avoided being a victim of industry consolidation. But dominance served to make them an attractive proposition for the country's largest brewery, one that didn't have Lambic in its portfolio: Artois/Interbrew.

Vanden Stock couldn't countenance selling a stake in his brewery to Artois when the idea was first pitched to him. But his son and nephew chipped away at him, and eventually sold Artois (which by now had renamed itself Interbrew) a 43% share in September 1989. The influence of Artois – particularly new marketing techniques – soon made Vanden Stock feel "a stranger in his own enterprise." [60]

Belle-Vue had been exposed to an "externally infected company culture that was no longer mine," he said, and when Artois wanted to increase their stake to 80%, and Roger and Philippe were in favour, the elder Vanden Stock put up little resistance. "[F]or me personally, it ended in a fracture between living and working," he said. "And that remains a very strange, completely contrarian sensation...something remains still unprocessed about the whole affair." [61]

Roger Vanden Stock's claims the day after the sale that Belle-Vue wouldn't leave Brussels and they wanted to "reactivate the Brussels character of our beers" were quickly disproved.[62] Brewing stopped in Molenbeek in 1992, and the Brussels-based brewery closed definitively soon after as operations were centralised in a new hi-tech brewery seven kilometres away in Flemish Sint-Pieters-Leeuw. [63]

However it ended, Constant Vanden Stock was proud of his at Belle-Vue: "What began as a beer merchant with a café, a handcart and two colleagues, finished in a small beer empire."[64] Navigating changing consumer tastes, economic upheaval, and two world wars, his innovations at Belle-Vue transformed Lambic production, and pushed traditional Lambic culture to the brink of catastrophe while exporting Belle-Vue Kriek around Europe. With Anderlecht he fulfilled boyhood dreams of footballing glory, even if some of those have an asterisk attached to them and several of his adversaries spit at the sound of his name.

Above all, by July 1991 Vanden Stock felt that he done right by his father: "However it goes in the future, the name Philemon Vanden Stock has been posthumously honoured day after day for half a century...The bitter death of my father was not in vain."[65]

✻ ✻ ✻

Postscript – February 23, 2020
It's match day in Brussels. A slow trickle of football fans passes by Café Belle-Vue. Inside, surrounded by obsolete Lambic paraphernalia, there is an occasional flash of subtle purple or the glimpse of the Anderlecht crest. They still serve Belle-Vue Kriek here, from a fake barrel with the words Lambic, Kriek and Framboise painted in whitewash on the wood.

The Vanden Stock stranglehold on Brussels has weakened. Philemon Vanden Stock's name is still visible above the café and the brewery, even if the family no longer owns the former and the brewery has been converted into a hotel and museum. In 2018 a Flemish entrepreneur took majority control of the football club. The grip of the Vande Stock family on Anderlecht football club was loosened definitively and permanently, when in 2019 the new owner made the decision to remove Constant Vanden Stock's name from the stadium in favour of a new club sponsor.

Once the fans here at Café Belle-Vue are finished with their smoked salmon and white wine, they will amble up the hill behind the café. There's little to remind today's younger match-goers of the dynasty built on the back of Brussels' largest brewery. But, after the mauve throng files in through the chipped green turnstiles of the newly-named Lotto Park, they might enjoy a Kriek or two with their football.

BUILD-A-BRAND

*The strange life, inevitable death, and
curious rebirth of Caulier*

Skieven Architek. Not many cities have a dedicated curse word for architects and malicious developers, but Brussels does. For locals it reflects their animosity towards the developers and urban planners who through their periodic, megalomaniacal plans to reinvent Brussels – the imperial power projections of Leopold II, 19th century public works, the ghastly reconfiguring of Brussels as a post-World War II car-centric city – have trampled on the city's residents for centuries. Brewers have suffered as much as anyone at the hands of these scheming architects. Whenever developers arrived in a neighbourhood, breweries were among the first businesses to fall victim to the wrecking ball of progress.

So when Eric Coppieters, the man behind the Caulier

Sugar Free beer brand, in an interview in December 2018 said that he "loves to build", the people of Brussels may be wary. Luckily for Coppieters, and Brussels, his intention was to build a brewery. Actually, rebuild is probably a better description because, in Coppieters' stated ambition to open a Caulier brewery in Brussels by 2021, he's bring a stalwart of 20th century Brussels brewing back to the city, and to Caulier's ancestral Brussels home 50 years after it was demolished.

Brewing on cobblestones

For nearly a century, Brasserie Caulier stood on Rue Herry, in the wedge of land hemmed in by the Brussels canal and the train tracks terminating in the Brussels North station. In Caulier's time, locals knew it as the kasseienwijk for the abundant cobbled streets.[66] This was a neighbourhood that would have thrummed with commercial activity - the jangle of streetcars, the thud-thud-thud of car wheels on cobbles, the parping foghorns of barges moored on the quays of the adjacent docks. The neighbourhood was alive with industry, with factories, warehouses, and artisan workshops.

Caulier was just one brewery of several to open in the kasseienwijk as Brussels beer experienced a boom in the last quarter of the 19th century. In 1893, the brothers Caulier inherited a business their grandfather had grown to include breweries in Brussels and in Wallonia. They consolidated this network of breweries under the banner of Caulier frères and Brussels – then the industrial heartland of Belgian brewing – became their base of operations. By the 1920s, the brewery included a six-vessel brewhouse, and 200 square tanks in the fermentation cellars. On this equipment, the brothers built Caulier's success, focusing on foreign beer styles – Bock, Double Bock, and the brewery's flagship, Perle Caulier 28.

Caulier 28, the pearl of beers

Dubbed "the pearl of beers", the 28 referred to a trick the brewery pulled to avoid paying additional excise duty. At the time, there was a special levy on beers brewed with more than 28 kilos of grain per 100 litres of water.[67] Spotting a marketing opportunity, and a chance to save money, the Caulier brothers brewed a quality beer to these exacting specifications. Perle Caulier 28 was the result, and the brewery plastered their iconic round logo with the number 28 all around Brussels.

As the brewery grew, the Caulier brothers kept it anchored to the kasseienwijk. Each evening, as the brewing day ended and the sweet smell of spent grain hung rich and thick in the air, farmers trekked their horses over the cobblestones and into Caulier's courtyard to collect steaming piles of spent grain to feed their animals. Locals were invited into Caulier each year for a party at the brewery's parquet-floored ballroom, to carouse on the account of the brewery's owners.

Elsewhere in the city, the brewery hired illustrious local architects to build their own pleasure palaces in which they sold Caulier beer to the locals. One such example - designed by Adrian Blomme, the architect of the landmark Wielemans-Ceuppens brewery in Vorst - is still standing today on the corner of Boulevard Lemonnier and Boulevard du Midi in the shadow of the Gare du Midi. Even though it's long since converted into a fast-food restaurant, Perle Caulier in bright blue ceramic tile still dominates the building's facade, alongside the iconic white "28" in a red circle logo of the brewery. [68]

Caulier's fatal decision

Caulier's location on the periphery of central Brussels spared it the upheaval faced by other breweries forced to relocate when the city centre was transformed by the burying of the Senne river underground from the 1870s onwards, and the later wholesale destruction caused by the construction of the north-south rail link that cut an unresolved psychic scar through the heart of the medieval core of Brussels. The brewery grew steadily in the first half of the 20th century, and after World War II, Caulier increasingly focused its energies in growing its exports to France and Germany.

But, in a hubristic decision in September 1960, Caulier's owners determined to bring their now-sprawling brewing empire under one roof in order to increase production to satisfy and expand these growing export markets. They chose the industrial village on Ghlin on the outskirts of Mons as the site of a new 27,000m2, 700,000-hectolitre brewery.[69]

The move to Ghlin was a failure for Caulier, which with the move rechristened itself Brasserie Ghlin in a complex corporate structure incorporated the original Brussels business and several other breweries they had acquired over the years. Caulier/Ghlin struggled through the economic downturn of the early 1970s, and after an abortive takeover by US brewery Schlitz intended to give that company a beachhead through which it attempted to sell American beer in the European market, the Belgian government was forced to rescue Ghlin in 1978.

The government negotiated a then-secret joint take-over by the Artois and Piedboeuf breweries – the first step to what would become Interbrew, and eventually AB Inbev. But even they couldn't save what was left of Caulier. When, in 1993 the Ghlin brewery complex in Ghlin bottled its last Jupiler and Interbrew shut it down, Caulier's history in the Brussels kasseienwijk was already a dimming folk memory.

Manhattan-on-the-Senne

The Caulier site in Brussels had continued to operate at a smaller scale after the opening of the Ghlin facility. When it eventually shut down around 1968, it was soon gobbled up into the maws of Brussels' rapacious nexus of developers and politicians. By the late 1960s, this group had spotted an opportunity in Caulier's hardscrabble neighbourhood. Light and heavy industry alike had abandoned this corner of Brussels in favour of less cramped lodgings outside the city, and the lower middle class had fled after them into the suburbs. In their stead came "guest workers" from Turkey and Morocco, moving in alongside pensioners and those who were too poor to escape the decrepitude facilitated by an indifferent - or worse - government.

The tenement housing declined to a parlous state, and with the construction of the new Brussels north train station in the late 1950s, the area was ripe for redevelopment. The neighbourhood between the canal and the station was lively but poor and politically disenfranchised, with little representation or voice in the face of Belgium's political-developer industry. In place of crumbling row houses and "arthouse cinemas", a cabal of developers and politicians around then-Belgian Prime Minister Paul Vanden Boynants dreamed of a car-centric business district packed with towering skyscrapers and pedestrians relegated to walkways high above street level. In 1967, Vanden Boynants and his acolyte

Charly de Pauw – a developer who went by the nick-
name "King Carpark" – announced their dream to the
world: The *Manhattenplan.* [70]

A Corbusian nightmare

It was a vision of rectilinear streets and buildings,
80 in total. There would even in time come a motorway interchange intended to link Brussels to the
then-emerging pan-European motorway network.
The crowing glory would be the World Trade Centre,
a series of office tower blocks originally planned
to be taller than their New York equivalents. As
part of the plan's rollout, the remaining industry
in the neighbourhood was demolished. A wrecking
crew came for the Caulier brewery in 1970 to put
an end to the brewery's association with Brussels.
Their dream of a Manhattan-on-the-Senne was, in
reality, a Corbusian nightmare. A down-at-heel com-
munity of poverty, lasciviousness and foreign workers was emptied and replaced by empty, windblown
boulevards flanked by identikit post-war apartment
blocks. Virtually all of the tenement housing, cafes,
cinemas, and sex shops that gave the neighbourhood
life vanished in the space of a decade. The wrecking
crews moved in even as residents were still living in
their homes or on the verge of eviction.

Today, only the cobblestones and a few tenement
row houses predating this scorched-earth policy remain. Rue Herry and the surrounding streets on

which the Caulier buildings were located were wiped off the map, and where they once stood is now a park given over to an informal camp for transit migrants in a brutalised neighbourhood bearing little resemblance to what came before.

And it was all for nothing, because the Manhattenplan was an unrealised failure.

It was crippled by economic crises throughout the 1970s before it ever really started. The motorway never came, nor did the skywalks for pedestrians. Of the eight World Trade Centre towers originally planned, only three were ever built. Even today, the city's planners and architects are working to undo the damage wrought by a generation of feckless political leadership. Despite the wholesale failure of the plan, the impulses that drove the destructive plan never really went away; instead, they slunk off into the shadows, waiting until more lucrative economic circumstances returned. [71]

Revenge of the developers
And returned they have. Brussels in 2019 is struggling with growing housing demand. Once again, the neighbourhoods around the Kasseienwijk and the opposite canal bank are humming with construction activity as developers work to make up the shortfall. Now though, they are working from a blank canvas, filling in the gashes in the urban landscape left behind by their bankrupted predecessors,

and there are no more breweries to demolish. Quite the contrary, in fact. The modern-day descendants of the developers that razed Caulier to the ground are increasingly attracted to businesses like breweries, considering their inclusion in new developments as one more – increasingly attractive – bauble to attract high-earning, young residents to unfashionable neighbourhoods. Exactly the kinds of places that Caulier once called home.

Enter Eric Coppieters, a builder of a different sort. Coppieters spent two decades in business, leading the international expansion of the Belgian restaurant chain Le Pain Quotidien, and chocolatier Pierre Marcolini. He didn't know much about brewing when he bought the right to use the Caulier 28 brand in 2009, but he did see an opportunity to re-launch Caulier as a low-calorie beer and capture the health-conscious, beer drinking market. "I'm quite sporty. I have a lot of friends like me who like to enjoy life and they don't want to put weight just for the sake of it. That's what got me in the project," he said in an interview with Brussels Beer City in December 2018.

Caulier's revival

Coppieters worked with Dirk Naudts of De Proefboruwerij and Belgian brewing eminence grise Willem van Herreweghe to hone the recipe for the new Caulier 28, and his team spent the first five years getting their marketing right. Coppieters took

over day-to-day management when a business partner left in 2013, and has guided Caulier's growth
strategy since. His approach is simple: target an
urban market, grow sales to 10,000 hectolitres, and
contract production locally. It's an approach that
led Coppieters to merge Caulier Sugar Free with Ital-
ian brewery Birrificio Toccalmatto in 2017, and to
launch plans to open a brewpub in Mexico City in
January 2020 (as of May 2020 there has been no offi-
cial announcement made about its opening). It was
always clear that the company couldn't contract
their beers to De Proef indefinitely, and Brussels had
been earmarked as the site of a new Caulier brewery
for some time.

According to Coppieters, he was in talks with Naudts
to open an extension of De Proef in Brussels for several years, anticipating that they would hit 10,000
hectolitres of sales in the Benelux by 2020. Naudts
eventually secured permission to expand his exist-
ing site, so Coppieters kept working on his Brussels
plans alone. "We had other possibilities for a location, but in the end we had a preference for going
back to the story of the brand," he says, even if the
Caulier of 2019 is a very different beast from its Brussels ancestor. Coppieters' first step in returning to
Brussels was to open a branch of the company's Bras-
serie28 chains in an old post office building adjacent
to Brussels' central station. He acquired in the summer of 2019 the lease of a long-defunct restaurant -

Maxim's - on the Grand Place, with the intention to open another brasserie-type venue.

The return of Caulier brewing to Brussels was secured when Coppieters was contacted by the company responsible for the redevelopment of the massive Tour & Taxis site next to the Brussels canal. He expects his 20,000-30,000 hectolitre brewery to be operational there by 2021, even if he didn't confirm exactly where it will be located. As of July 2019, Coppieters' company announced it was on track to open a 20,000 hectolitre capacity brewery at Tour & Taxis by the end of 2020. It remains to be seen what impact the Covid-19 crisis will have on these plans.

Formerly the goods terminal of the Thurn und Taxis postal company, the collection of Victorian-era warehouses, goods sheds, and jumble of other industrial buildings that make up the Tour & Taxis site has been under development since 2000. Its current owners are eager to ensure a healthy mix of residential, office, and light industrial activity on the site; and breweries fit that brief perfectly. And, unlike their 1960s equivalents, Brussels' current generation of urban planners and city administrators think the same.

Brewing in Brussels is back – and so is Caulier
They have worked hard to show that productive industries still have an important place in the city, and they have supported breweries in finding space

and financing to stay in the city in the hope that breweries could in the future provide low-skilled industrial jobs in an area of Brussels that has struggled with chronic unemployment ever since the previous generation of Brussels breweries and the rest of the city's industry vanished in the 1960s and 1970s.

The breweries, at least, are now returning. Many of them are heading to Tour & Taxis. En Stoemelings and No Science have been operating close to Tour & Taxis since 2017. Brasserie de la Senne completed a purpose-built brewery there in late-2019 complete with a new tap room, and La Source Beer Co. opened in October 2019 in a shared space with a fermentation workshop. Even Brussels Beer Project was offered a site there – next to de la Senne – but turned it down in favour of another canal-side location further west.

Coppieters is sanguine about competing with his future neighbours. "Brussels should be able to have a craft local beer market of 200,000-300,000 hectolitres in the future. To have Brasserie de la Senne, Brussels Beer Project and us in a five kilometre [radius], it will be a good tourist attraction," he said. "There is really room enough for all three, and we all have our specific orientation...It's really possible to do a good job together."

* * *

Returning to equilibrium

In the original Caulier's heyday, most of the beer sold in Brussels was brewed in Brussels. Brewing in the city may never reach those levels again, but Coppieters confidence that there's enough room for everyone is not misplaced. After a period of tumultuous and at times cataclysmic change, Brussels brewing is again inching back to some kind of equilibrium. His Caulier may be an outlier in the Brussels scene – too much business and not enough romanticism. But, the story of Caulier's birth, death, and strange revival is a good indication of the place of beer in Brussels in 2020.

Beer is relevant again to Brussels in a way that it hasn't been for half a century. It's no longer just a part of the past, but is an urgent part of the city's present and future – essential to conversations about localism and the place of industry in a densely populated city. By convincing Brussels' cadre of developers of their worth, the city's brewers have insulated themselves from the capricious swing of the wrecking ball. For now, at least, breweries in Brussels have nothing to fear from Skieven Architeks.

EPILOGUE

In search of lost beers

I t's a Sunday in February and I'm on a mission: to drink a beer from each of the last four centuries of Brussels brewing history. I've arranged to meet with author Joe Stange, a reliable Sancho Panza for this adventure, at Brussels literary café Le Fleur en Papier Doré. I've chosen this café because it is usually reliable in having the four beers on my list – a draught Boon Lambic, Cantillon Gueuze, CTS Scotch, and Zinnebir from Brasserie de la Senne.

Kaleidoscopic choice

Writing about beer history can be frustrating. Most of the breweries I write about are gone, as are the beers they made. And, according to Yvan De Baets, old beer recipes aren't enough to bring them back: "I understand the fantasy but that's the real fantasy. You need the whole brewery, and the brewers. I wish it was the case, but sadly it's not," says the co-founder of Brasserie de la Senne.

Which is a shame because, much like today's craft beer drinker, an 1880s café-goer in Brussels could choose from a kaleidoscopic mix of beers: lambic, Leuvensch wheat beer, or even a Bavarian Salvator. While I'll never know how these tasted, there are beers that have survived to tell a story about brewing in each of the last four centuries, and all should be available at La Fleur en Papier Doré.

Joe's there when I arrive, but immediately disaster strikes. A waitress informs me they've run out of lambic. I have to skip ahead a century and order a Cantillon Gueuze instead, a neat illustration of how gueuze came to eclipse its elder sibling.

"The spirit of Brabant"
Gueuze was an attempt to produce a domestic rival to clear, sparkling, and not sour beers imported from England and Germany. Brewers had experimented with bottled Lambic as far back as the 1840s, but Geuze really took off from the 1890s, slowly supplanting lambic and faro as Brussels' default spon-

taneously fermented beer. A blend of aged lambics refermented in the bottle, Geuze was, in the words of Flemish poet Hubert van Herreweghen, "a product of the soil and spirit of Brabant". [72]

Post-WWII gueuze splintered into the ascetic tradition represented by Cantillon, and the Belle-Vue's industrial interpretation. The former won out, barely; by the 1990s, Cantillon was the only Brussels gueuze brewery of any sort left. Which is why I can enjoy the beautifully tart glass of gueuze sitting in front of me.

Gueuze finished, my poorly constructed plan falls again at the next hurdle. They've taken CTS Scotch off the menu. Instead, I jump ahead to 2004 and to Brasserie de la Senne's Zinnebir. The brewery, founded by De Baets and his partner Bernard Leboucq marked the reversal of a decades-long exodus of breweries from Brussels. And Zinnebir was their flagship, a floral, rounded, bitter Pale Ale that – like so many of its predecessors – took its lead from traditional English beer styles.

Musing on the impact of de la Senne on the contemporary beer scene, Joe says that Zinnebir established a new Brussels style: the Brussels pale ale. Dry, pale, bitter, balanced, and most importantly "doordrinkbaar", drinkable – almost every Brussels brewery has their analogue.

At Les Brasseurs

Joe and I strategise about where to find the missing beers. There is one obvious contender: Les Brasseurs on Boulevard Anspach. We traipse downtown, and as expected, there on the bar is a facsimile Lambic barrel perched on the bar. The history of Lambic is of cod history and mythology – the origin of the name, how old it really is, how much it has changed. What's less in doubt is that it was the dominant beer in Brussels in the 18th and 19th centuries, and until the arrival of foreign beer styles in the 1850s, it was simply the beer that every brewery made.

Unblended Lambic, and Faro – a blend of equal parts lambic and meerts beer, sweetened at the café – vied to be the most popular beer among the drinking classes. Ultimately, though, they both disappeared as tastes in Brussels moved from tartness to sweetness. No one produces traditional faro, and lambic is only available in a few bars around the city. Les Brasseurs is one, pouring Boon instead of Cantillon. It's served to me in a traditional grey and blue ceramic jug – sweet, gently sour, and barely sparkling.

My hopes are raised on seeing draught CTS Scotch on the menu, but are quickly dashed by the barman who informs me that they, too are out. Joe and I part ways, and I consider my options. CTS Scotch comes from a now-unloved period in Brussels beer history when, pre-WWII, brewing industrialised and gravitated towards British styles. It was the era of the Navy's Christmas Ale, the Stout Vandenheuvel, and the CTS Scotch of Wielemans-Ceuppens. Of all these beers, only CTS Scotch survived post-war industry consolidation – even if AB Inbev in Leuven now brews it.

Scotched

It then hits me. What better find a former Wielemans beer than in a former Wielemans café? That's how I find myself several days later sat on an orange banquette in the Café Metropole, a raisin-brown glass of CTS Scotch in hand. The Wielemans brothers opened the café in the 1890s, but there is very little evidence today that brewers built it. The menu consists of AB InBev staples, which does at least meet my needs. Sadly, after the effort I've gone to find it, the beer itself is little more than a historical curiosity. When I take a sup, it offers not much more than a hint of liquorice, burnt sugar and butterscotch.

Much like Café Metropole, the beer has presumably seen better days. And while you patch up the flaking plasterwork of the former, you're never going to be able recreate the CTS Scotch of its heyday. There is probably not much point anyway; 21st century tastes in Brussels have moved on, and nowadays, it's a historical footnote, one more faddish beer from a previous century whose target audience is no more. I pour one out for four centuries of brewing history.

ACKNOWLEDGE-
MENTS

This book would not exist without Paul Walsh, who took a punt on an article I wrote in the summer of 2017 and spun it out to a series of beer history articles in Belgian Beer and Food Magazine. Unfortunately the idea outlived the magazine, but I'm hugely grateful for the opportunities he gave me to write about what I love.

To others at Belgian Beer and Food Magazine – John Rega, Breandán Kearney, and Joe Stange – thanks for your constantly encouraging words, and for not being mad at me taking up space in the magazine. Particular thanks to Joe, who has been an invaluable sounding board for ideas over copious glasses, for his openness in sharing his knowledge and sources about Brussels and its beer, and for agreeing to write the foreword to this without a moment's hesitation.

To everyone online and offline who has been an inspiration (knowingly or otherwise) and a goal for me, who have supported Brussels Beer City from the beginning, reading and sharing my articles, and who have paid me occasionally to write for you – Adrian Tierney-Jones, Pete Browne, Luc de Raedemaeker, Matthew Curtis, Jonny Hamilton, Jef Van Den Steen, Ciara Kenny, Ben Keene, Boak and Bailey, Lily Waite, Stan Hieronymus, Katie Mather, Claire Bullen, and Richard Croasdale.

Thanks to Sam and Lauren for reading a draft of this book, giving me positive feedback just when I needed it, and not throwing it back in my face. To Jonny and Claire for their kind words, and to Adrian for his thorough line-by-line proofreading.

Thank you to everyone who sat down for an interview with me for the articles – those quoted and not – including Yvan De Baets, Eric Coppieters, Guido Vanderhulst, Anne Tollet. To Dries Plevoets and Marianne de Fossé for facilitating my visit to Brasseries Atlas. The articles included in this collection could not have been written without the essential work done by Guy Moerenhout, Patricia Quintens, Michaël Bellon, La Fonderie, Bruxelles Fabriques, the people behind the Musée Schaerbeekois de la Bière, BRASS, and Adam, Bill and the Lambic.Info crew.

Thanks to Thierry Van Linthoudt for letting me spend a couple of hours rummaging around his vast collection of books, glasses, and memorabilia spanning a century and more of Belgian brewing. To Jo Panneels for pointing me in the direction of useful source materials.

Huge thanks to Ruairí for his design work

To Noa and Zoey for accommodating their dad's bierwerk. And to Lore, thanks for staying put for the late nights and long hours with me spent in the basement or in the kitchen, for reviewing each and every article honestly and brutally, and for pushing me forward when I faltered.

ABOUT THE AUTHOR

A ward-winning beer writer, Eoghan Walsh founded the website Brussels Beer City in 2017. In 2018, he was awarded the Best Young Beer Writer by the British Guild of Beer Writers. He has won silver and bronze medals for his beer writing by the North American Guild of Beer Writers.

Eoghan's work has featured in Belgian Beer and Food Magazine, Good Beer Hunting, Ferment, and The Irish Times.

Originally from Ireland, he has lived in Brussels since 2009.

NOTES

[1] *Bier et Brouwerijen te Brussel*, Patricia Quintens, AMVB, 1996

[2] "NOUVEAU: La Brasserie De Boeck à Koekelberg", *C'était au temps où Bruxelles brassait*, Guy Moerenhout, February 9 2009: https://biereetbrasseriesbruxelles.wordpress.com/2009/02/09/ nouveau-la-brasserie-de-boeck-a-koekelberg/

[3] Quintens, 1996

[4] *Tome II - Les vieux estaminets de Bruxelles et environs*, Robert Desart & Marinus, Albert (préface)

[5] *Brussels: A cultural and literary history*, André De Vries, Signal Books, 2002

[6] *Koekelberg Au fil du temps... Au coeur des rues...*, Didier Sutter, Drukker, 2012

[7] Sutter, 2012

[8] Quintens, 1996

[9] Sutter, 2012

[10] Sutter, 2012

[11] Sutter, 2012

[12] Sutter, 2012

[13] Sutter, 2012

[14] "NOUVEAU: La Brasserie De Boeck à Koekelberg", Guy moerenhout https://biereetbrasseriesbruxelles.wordpress.com/2009/02/09/ nouveau-la-brasserie-de-boeck-a-koekelberg/

[15] "Koekelberg - Fin des espoirs pour le site De Boeck Démolition

annoncée" Fabrice Voogt, *Le Soir*, June 23, 2003: https://www.lesoir.be/art/%252Fkoekelberg-fin-des-espoirs-pour-le-site-de-boeck-demoli_t-20030623-Z0N8WY.html

[16] "La brasserie Atlas à Anderlecht", *C'était au temps où Bruxelles brassait*, Guy Moerenhout, April 10, 2006: https://biereetbrasseriesbruxelles.wordpress.com/2006/04/10/la-brasserie-atlas-a-anderlecht/

[17] "Brouwerij Atlas: Industrialisering van een sector", *Erfgoed Brussel N° 015-016*, Marianne Fossé, 2015: http://erfgoed.brussels/links/digitale-publicaties/pdf-versies/artikels-van-het-tijdschrift-erfgoed-brussel/nummer-15-16/artikel-15-16-5

[18] "Anderlecht: nieuwe stadswijk aan kanaaloevers", *Bruzz*, May 7 2012:
https://www.bruzz.be/samenleving/anderlecht-nieuwe-stadswijk-aan-kanaaloevers-2012-05-07

[19] "Plaisirs d'Expo: La Belgique "joyeuse" et les joyeux Belges..." Valérie Piette, *Les Cahiers de La Fonderie 37: Exposition universelle 58*, La Fonderie, 2007

[20] Quintens, 1996

[21] "C'était au temps où Bruxelles inventait (I): Vandenheuvel La Stout et l'Export ont fait mousser les estaminets", Le Soir, Sylvie Lausberg, August 3 1999: https://www.lesoir.be/art/c-etait-au-temps-ou-bruxelles-inventait-i-vandenheuvel-_t-19990803-Z0H2WQ.html

[22] *La fabrication moderne de la bière*, Brasserie Vandenheuvel, 1955

[23] *Expo 58 en zijn bierbrouwers*, François Van Kerckhoven, boekscout.nl, 2013.

[24] Van Kerckhoven, 2013

[25] "The Britannia, Brussels, 1958", *Boak and Bailey*, June 24 2014: https://boakandbailey.com/2014/06/britannia-brussels-1958/

[26] Piette, 2007

[27] "La brasserie de la semaine: Wielemans a Forest" *C'était au temps où Bruxelles brassait*, Guy Moerenhout, August 30, 2004: http://biere-et-brasseries-bruxelles.skynetblogs.be/archive/2004/08/30/la-brasserie-de-la-semaine-wielemans-a-forest-1.html

[28] "Wielemans-Ceuppens: Grandeur et decadence d'une brasserie", Jean-Paul Vaes, *Les Cahiers de la Fonderie: Biéres Brasseries Patrimoine Industriel*, La Fonderie, 1990

[29] Vaes, 1990

[30] Vaes, 1990

[31] *La Revue Documentaire: Organe mensuel de l'industrie du batiment*, Etablissement Henri badoux, July 15 1931 http://monuments.tipos.be/opac_css/doc_num.php?explnum_id=61

[32] Vaes, 1990

[33] *W: Zeven wandelingen rondom Wielemans-Ceuppens*, Zimmerfrei, Wiels, 2013

[34] "Wielemans-Ceuppens - Le métier de maitre brasseur: Entretien avec Martin Vandenborre", *Les Cahiers de la Fonderie: Biéres Brasseries Patrimoine Industriel*, La Fonderie, 1990

[35] Ibid

[36] "Bruxelles en mouvements: N°164 – 13 avril 2006", *Bruxelles en mouvements* , IEB, April 13 2006: http://www.ieb.be/IMG/pdf/bem164_13042006-2.pdf

[37] "La Fonderie veut sauver", Guido Vanderhulst, *Les Cahiers de la Fonderie: Biéres Brasseries Patrimoine Industriel*, La Fonderie, 1990

[38] *Wielemans Machines*, accessed March 6 2019: https://www.wielemansmachines.com/

[39] Quintens, 1996

[40] "La Brasserie de la semaine: leopold a Ixelles", *C'était au temps où Bruxelles brassait*, Guy Moerenhout, July 6, 2004: https://biereetbrasseriesbruxelles.wordpress.com/2004/07/06/la-brasserie-de-la-semaine-leopold-a-ixelles/

[41] *Constant vanden Stock: Een leven, twee carriers*, Hugo Camps,

Kritak/Thomas Rap, 1993

[42] Camps, 1993

[43] Camps, 1993

[44] Camps, 1993

[45] Camps, 1993

[46] Camps, 1993

[47] *Geuze & Kriek*, Jef Vanden Steen, Lannoo, 2011

[48] Camps, 1993

[49] "Weg van Lambiek", *Bruzz*, November 16 2007, https://www.bruzz.be/samenleving/weg-van-lambiek-2007-11-16

[50] Camps, 1993

[51] Camps, 1993

[52] "Bribed in Brussels: How Nottingham Forest fell victim to fixing scandal", Daniel Taylor, The Guardian: December 11, 2013 https://www.theguardian.com/football/blog/2013/dec/11/nottingham-forest-anderlecht-match-fixing-scandal-1984

[53] Taylor, 2013

[54] "CONSTANT VANDEN STOCK A RECONNU LA CORRUPTION ROGER VANDEN STOCK:MON PERE S'EST TU POUR ME PROTEGER UN MILLION A L'ARBITRE..." Jean-Louis Donnay et Frédéric Larsimont, *Le Soir*, September 5 1997: https://www.lesoir.be/art/%252Fconstant-vanden-stock-a-reconnu-la-corruption-roger-van_t-19970905-Z0E5U4.html

[55] "Uefa had Forest-Anderlecht referee bribe evidence 'for four years'", *BBC*, September 25 2016: https://www.bbc.com/news/uk-england-nottinghamshire-37453762

[56] "SUR LE RACHAT DE LA BRASSERIE BELLE-VUE PAR LE GROUPE INTERBREW", Christian Laporte, *Le Soir*, July 5, 1991: https://plus.lesoir.be/art/d-19910705-W3KN00

[57] Camps, 1993

[58] Camps, 1993

[59] Camps, 1993

[60] Camps, 1993

[61] Camps, 1993

[62] Laporte, 1991

[63] Quintens, 1996

[64] Camps, 1993

[65] Camps, 1993

[66] *Van vergane glorie: de verdwenen brouwerijen van Laken*, Eric Christiaens & Wim van der Elst, Laca: http://www.laken-ingezoomd.be/magazine/201112131226_LT %2020%20Brouwerijen.pdf

[67] "Brasserie Caulier – partie I: les sièges de Neufvilles et Mons", *C'était au temps où Bruxelles brassait*, Guy Moerenhout, May 24 2005: https://biereetbrasseriesbruxelles.wordpress.com/2005/05/24/brasserie-caulier-partie-i-les-sieges-de-neufvilles-et-mons/

[68] Christiaens & van der Elst

[69] *De Brouwerij van Ghlin*, Brasserie du Ghlin, 1962

[70] Quintens, 1996

[71] "Balans van 45 jaar Noordwijk", Steven Van Garsse, Bruzz, April 1 2011: https://www.bruzz.be/samenleving/balans-van-45-jaar-noordwijk-2011-04-01

[72] *Geuze en Humanisme: zelfgenoegzame beschouwingen over de voortreffelijkheid van het bier van Brussel en Brabant en van de mensen die het drinken*, Hubert van Herreweghen, P Uitgeverij, 1955

About the author

George spent many years investigating real cases of child abuse in the Metropolitan Police Service. In between writing and walking his beloved dog, he continues to work helping young people in Surrey.

WHO NEEDS FLOWERS WHEN
THEY'RE DEAD?